T0359839

Subliminal Dust

POOJA MITTAL

First published by Odyssey Books in 2010

Copyright © Pooja Mittal 2010

Odyssey Books Pty Ltd
PO Box 1152, Fyshwick ACT 2609
www.odysseybooks.com.au

National Library of Australia
Cataloguing-in-Publication entry

Author:	Mittal, Pooja
Title:	Subliminal dust / Pooja Mittal
ISBN:	9780980690903 (pbk.)
Dewey Number:	NZ821.3

Cover artwork by Rin Gristwood

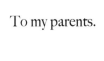
To my parents.

Poems

the veil 1

sound (& silence) 5

to adam 6

bouquet 9

to the scientist 10

as if nothing were born 12

perpetua 14

(no)vocaine 15

sleep 16

withdrawal 17

letters from van gogh 18

tsunami 20

confession 22

birds 23

equinox 24

seducing a poem 26

then 29

the night dances 30

dismemberment 32

dichotomy 34

sagano 36

voices, whispers 37

bloom 38

answer 39

painter 40

sandrock 41

too fond 42

two thousand 43

nightchild 44

familiar 45

gilt trip 46

sister 47

turandot 48

spires 51

hunger 52

tavern 53

visitor to ward 9 54

glass 55

sunrise 56

ode to ruffles 57

friend 60

aubade at city diner 61

wander 62

rehabilitation 63

haiku #1: crystal 66

rose 67

you forget my name. 67

mayur 68

ghat 70

haiku #2: glimmer 74

the woman & death 75

vigil 76

stone 77

dowry 78

proselyte 79

haiku #3: violets 80

cherub 81

poetics of solitude   82

kirsome   83

departure   84

kingfishers   86

pale green   87

boat in echuca   88

city verge   89

pyre   92

petal   93

bear   94

forget   95

list of replicates   96

b(i)rth   98

sweatshop blues   100

burn   101

seaworthy   102

the sun still rises   104

bushwalk   106

shape-shifter's song   107

sundress   108

exodus   109

taxonomy   110

pilgrim   116

gratitude   117

politics of the chair   118

the visit   120

organism   122

waiting (for dickinson)   124

coupling   125

four meditations (on silence & night)   126

the veil

"on a morning like any other," they say
           but they mean *in* a morning
because you're always
                        in a morning
            aren't you?

& so, *in* a morning like any other
           it occurred to me
                      quite suddenly
                           that I was opaque
& that a body was merely a curtain
 between two voids, both of which
           were unknown   & remained uncharted.
(the hearts of uncarved birds.)

this morning, you see, was so
           gloriously ordinary, ordinary as an orange
& speckled as one, built of infinite pores
           that breathed in air
                      & breathed out
                                      fog.
           a citrus tinge
coloured the sky & rendered it finite, gave
the pock-marked canvas a certain
                      three
dimensionality. (birds, distant as freckles,
                 marring otherwise smooth
           skin.)

there are skies & then there are *skies*,
if you catch my meaning—there are skies
that gleam like boiled eggs

   or bald pates,
that crack themselves open
on the horizon & other inconsiderately
     sharp
    landmarks. (trees, telegraph poles,
      raised hands.) there are skies
that open up & keep on opening, blue lotuses
    almost vehement
        in their surrender.
there are skies that should know better,
    that cloak themselves despite fair weather,
     suspicious
as high-collared detectives, goggled
    as disgruntled pilots. & there are skies
that nestle, kept animals, fur bristle-smooth
    under the broad bright palm
     of the sun. but *this*,
this morning, was terribly unremarkable
    especially after the rain.

there was nothing to it. soggy as a child's
sock, a sky filled with pebbles
    each cloud rounder than the one before it
& gleaming
     stubborn
    as a delinquent's eye. in the long spaces
between them, the sky rippled (citrus) & the birds
drifted downwards (bits of ash).

    & on this morning
the earth was somehow oblivious:
    a heavy sleeper, turning
     wide-hipped (hills, townships)
under the pale, shaggy coverlet
    of dawn. I nestled in its lap, a cuckoo's child

in a nest not rightfully its own,
but still warm, so warm, the feathered weight
of mother-bosom upon me.

I was a body.   smaller than
more exquisite than
more delicious than
the citrus morning itself. I was
a little knot, a pulsing clot, a clenched fist
of flesh (slowly relaxing),
pursed as a mouth
or a rosebud is, incongruous, solid, primeval,
infantile. I was a child. I was a body.
I was the body of a child. I was punctuation.

between two great spaces, two great sentences,
what absurd curlicue
was I?
what pause did I give the vast churning
of the world? (inexorable as a garbage truck,
making mulch of what was once dead.)
this trundle & gurgle & silent heave
of a million infinitesimal things,
& I a million times *more* infinitesimal,
crouched between the dew-moist thighs
of a sleeping, adoptive mother:
looking up at a sky whose mere freckles
were far vaster than I. starburst, cellular,
photogenic. a face too small
to be noticed
without a grand
gasping
microscope. (sun-mirror burnished,
angled upon me in a sudden blaze of heat.)

oh, microscopic things. oh, living things.
          oh, dead things
                    & carried things
                             & given things
& birds in foreign skies. come down,
          with your scent
                    of old cigarettes
                             & fresh scandal, of new blood
          & ancient fossils. my bones mark the carbon
lines that will mark the stones
                    that will mark the place
          the hidden space
                    where you grow.

oh, living things.
                    we are opaque,
          our bodies merely a curtain
between two voids, both of which
                    are unknown   & remained uncharted.
(the hearts of uncarved
                            birds.)

sound (& silence)

terrible silences speak to me—
terribly pale silences, soft as the faces of new pigeons.
under the arch of an upturned sky
the rain collecting (wet-feathered coin-glitter)
in endless gutters.
slow aggregate of things
that shine, that refuse to shine.
breaths suspended, crossed arms of branches
suddenly deprived of clothing—
the nude earth
aching
like a young bride.

stripped & open, foot & soil
indistinguishable from mind—this downpour relentless
as the clatter of abandoned weapons. knife-quick,
bird-voices hide & reveal themselves.
sleight of hand, a shifting veil,
a stifled breath, a touch withdrawn.
terrible silences. across chasms of nearness,
between blades of grass, these silences
speak to me—agonisingly thin
as the voices of infants, all-encompassing as dusk,
merciless as dawn.

to adam

we are but pouches of skin
(porous bubbles) velveteen &
knuckles grafted from the roots of trees,
our hair a mat of leaves, the squirrel-fur
of old grass & our beaten palms
pressed against it, as if
in supplication.

& you ask me,
beloved, you ask me
where is our God?

when you touch my breasts
or my feet, there is
no worship in you, only
a clean song, the cleanest song
as of a flute
carved of bone.
you are empty, my love, of
thought. (you are full
of God.)

& so I say to you, beloved, there is
(where is) there is
our God: in the waxen gleam
of that not given to us, the wound
you leave in me, the flitting memory
of each scale you pick from my skin,
pebbles from a lake, silver & solitary,
none remembering
that they were once
part of a whole.

but you, picked from the skin of God, & I
cannot hear each other,
for neither remembers
that we were part of a whole. & so
you touch my back. guess at
the shape of my bones. & you ask me,
beloved, you ask me
where is our God?

your hands, when they open,
carry the shadow of rain. (you smell
of God.) moisture that makes of your limbs
a moss for me to slip against.
your mouth, when it opens, is a fruit
ripe with the harvests
of centuries past. (you taste
of God.)

& so I say to you, beloved, there is
(where is) there is
our God: in the sky always open above us,
relentless as a skein of silk
stretching into the abyss. there is
our God, in the islands beneath leaves,
in the furrows beneath eyes, in the shifts
beneath skin, in the muscle & the tone,
in the mind & the music
of knowing & naming things.

but you, who was first known & named
& I, that followed after, cannot know or name
each other. & so

you measure the heights of the skies, the depths
of the furrows, build bridges
between the islands, & you ask me,
beloved, you ask me
where is our God?
yet you, yourself, are measured & built
& sounded out, from the hull of your flank
to the sails of your lungs, song-filled. (you are known
by God.) but still you search. & within me
you cut new scores, making of the wood
of my skin your writing-board,
your knees against my stomach, your ink
upon my back.

you write me
until you know all my compositions,
until you have made of me
a clean song, the cleanest song
as of a flute
carved of bone.
I am empty, my love,
of thought. (I am full
of You.)

& so I say to You, beloved, there is
(where is) there is
our God.

bouquet

the roses line up
        tender as a funeral
                & heavy as
        red gauze
over the eyes of the dead.
                their scent a soft bomb
(as of cloves, leaves)
        fists unfurling under the earth
                giving of themselves
like widowed brides, all chiffon & silk.
leaden & light
        coffins of perfume
                pearlesque, encased
        in flesh. in their glow, candles stutter
as breaths do, feet fall
        as whispers do, accumulating secrets
with lips forever closed:
        divine closets
                of stubborn heat,
                        infinite shadows
                of coolness.
they curve & cup & part (mouths, thighs)
        with tongues of night-honey,
                the stir of a breeze
                        at dizzying heights.
touch them, know them, for they are skins
        not unlike our own:
                unbroken
                        but for a sigh
    of silence.
                darling, may our passing
                      be just as
                              gentle.

to the scientist

so many chromosomes. so many black dots
        under a microscope. hair follicles. stars.
this rough-spun cloth. freckles.
your science is sweet, so sweet, so foolish, I love you.
I love watching it bloom, a mad flower, & it thinks it wins,
& here you are, running quickly behind it
        a child behind a kite.
catch it catch it. it's new every time.

        then. silence.

you fight over it. I sit here, I'm sipping my coffee,
it's cold
        & you're
                fighting.
me? it? yourself? such sweet logic you have,
    illogical one. your wings kiss the sky;
   you measure the spoon in oceanfuls.
We can do it. We can do it. it's all numbers. & so
                  are you.

thinking is a waste of time. come play
        with me. let's pin it down, this blade of grass,
let's make it sing. so many green secrets. & us, too,
        & our arms, & our tongues, & our feet
that tread water so gently. *I think we used to be children.*
        I think we are.

there is music in this triangle. as in
        a shell.
                        listen to it.
listen to its angles, its equalness, its black lines that walk
so steadily. is there grammar? does it make sense? *Yes. Yes.*
            no. no. come play with me.
the beach is long & white—
        it is your arm, I sift the sand of it
& the sea
        comes in to crash.
                come play.

as if nothing were born

she spoke as if nothing were born
as if nothing could come forth
as if nothing could fail
            or succeed
in life's slow increments, heavy
as drops of mercury, the weight
            of a stillborn child.
the gentle inclination of a departing
back, the rust-hued sun, the freckles
that blossomed humble as daisies
on her daughter's face: the shapes
of those things were shrouded now,
as if behind a thousand
gauzy curtains
            numbed
by light. so beautiful the room
in which they took him from her.
this new son, now old as a kept thing,
a wrinkled antique, a pouch of skin—
an ancient, withered seed
torn out of its soil. only she
remained, alone in her body,
her blood & breath
            unshared. only she
remained, a single heart
                        beating
like a gong, a metronome,
its accompanying score
performed in silence. on the way back
from the hospital, the rain-wet road
gleamed as if it were a tongue

that had never known
        thirst. & she spoke
as if none of this were real,
as though the gullies & pot-holes
were craters on some distant moon
        unreachable
               except by the gods.

perpetua

the long, pale, solitary march
of your throat, wing-swept, blue as a dragon's tongue.
poison in small snifters; careful feet; pages removed
& replaced.

I do not ask you where you went.
I do not ask the how or why.

in the intent of your eye, that gleams
as a dulled blade does, lies my answer.
method & science, both contained in you
as if you were an elixir, a skin-clasped chalice,
your mind the fluid from which none dare drink.

stay silent, then.

in my palm I will carry away the seeds of your thoughts
& plant them elsewhere, where they will blossom
blue-tongued & gentle, so that other hands
may flinch away from them, so that another's water
may darken.

(no)vocaine

transparent blue shade of fallen & young things
       sky-tilt thru black glass
limbs (pale poppies) & mouths soft as dirt.
red where hip meets thigh. oh, darkness. clinging still
to sheet & lamp
       streak of knife-light
           where the curtains part.

where you go, I am not.

sleep

sleep does not come
to the waking—but the waking
come upon sleep, as upon
a body, mid-path, a soft occlusion
between sand & foot. some kneel
to feel it out, with their palms & mouths,
as if paying homage
to a beloved shape once departed
& now returned. others tread on it,
as on a leaf, a mere thin thing on a path
to a determined place, unwanted
as the hunger
of a stranger
one cannot feed.

withdrawal

agony room. the purpose of truth
is to mellow it down. green leaves.
if I am your equation, blue, come & seek me out—
here I am, heart open & eyes hungry;
I survey the land of you, I plant my seed.
I am not afraid. I am.

plaid. your skirt: casts shadow
of tree & vein upon your thigh.
such a grey room—why you lie in it, o girl of colour?
red girl, blue—why you raise your gun,
your empty throat, & why you fire fire fire?
what truth shall emerge from you?
you weave a fabric of pale lies—
your eyes tell it, they do.
your wings have long since
given up on you. free angel.
sit you in this room—wait you here.
wait you—
as if I would come for you—
as if—
& if I wasn't hungry, I wouldn't.
I wouldn't.

& then you laugh softly.
"But you are."

letters from van gogh

carcasses of stars, beached whales
the rock of night
        dashed against
                dashed against

        *

        wild fists of wind
beating the bright sun-drum

        *

the stars a single angry scratch
screaming
        LOVE LOVE LOVE
& beneath that the steep cliff
bottoming out into nothingness
with the city lights bobbing like baubles
        oh oh the singular jazz
            the rough hay
of awoken light—the rude bird, the broken lamp
the shoe still clinging to the earth
        the bright mind
                taking off

        *

your yellow really should know better
it isn't thick enough
with my fingers spanning your wrist
        what, what pulse
            can you give me?

your drooping head, your mad hair
the cut veins of your limbs—
I wrap & wrap the light around you
like a splint
            but you can't
                        simply can't
uphold yourself
you fool
you are a wire chair
you are a hidden fright
            you are
                        you are
what you are
I am not

                        *

the artisan doesn't like white
because white is plaster, white
            is death
white is the finishing touch
when all other touches
            have come & gone.
the violet with its timid hair
& over there, blue curled up
like an abandoned child
but the lone eye, with its pallid white,
            is inconsolable—
bread touches skin touches starvation
white is the taste
            of an abandoned house
white is the arch
            before it falls.

tsunami

lake, the shape of a glutton's stomach.
the defencelessness of human bodies,
pouch-heavy & filled with dirt:
mouths with water, hearts with sand.

bone-flutes & rattle toys, cats picking
through them like anxious mothers
looking for lice. strands of water brushed
aside by tree-fingers, telephone poles—
tall wavering shadows
as placid as towers.

rats huddle in shivering fists of skin,
haunches like the balls of thumbs—
knuckled hands cut off from bodies & clinging,
desperately, to the edge of a dangling drainpipe
or the triangular precipice of an upturned roof.

there, the sullen dog minds his shadow—
scarpers sideways along a fallen tree,
a lone, bedraggled bishop in a deserted
congregation. pews of river-ripple
empty: only a few sleeping faces, folded like cloth,
lids puffed & mouths blue. lilacs blooming on
floating arms. bruised aureoles
pollinated by small, buzzing things.

windows glisten in the distance, perforated
wings: sky-veined, moth-thin. almost thinner
than light. a single cylinder of steel,
partly submerged, surfaces from the water
as a gleaming curve: a perfect fingernail
pointing upwards, to a shoe on a broken sill.
(square of unidentifiable fabric
sewn on the instep.)

the silence, glass-heavy, is dusted by motes.
smudges of cloud. translucent, crystal shadows
that sail by like ships. no question, no answer.

no signal; no noise.

confession

it's not like I don't know.
if only you'd waited
by the traffic lights in your
silly flowers of shoes,
you'd know. the carousel
never stops. your skirt
with its full-time job
of fielding gazes blooms,
unfurls in the wind,
a red petal. it's monstrous
that you don't know.
the parking signs don't
say it, but the lizard
in all its gleaming patience
knows. eternity waits
for no one. your silly
shoes, the traffic lights.
those cars in their little
bubbles of blue. I loved
you long before the reviews
came out, your photos,
your hair. it's not like I
don't know. if only you'd
waited, lizard-like, by
the black tangle of graffiti
outside your flat, you'd know.

birds

a black heron treads
the great white beaches
of your brow
& upon your hands
rest the small lights
of stars, distant as dust.
to know infinity is to know
how to measure the finite,
refuse to measure it,
the voices of night in E flat & A
minor: slow doves above
      a cacophony
           of silence.

equinox

shades of frost, grey & disconnected,
gleam on the eaves of dusk. (dark, elaborate,
limned with curves. clouds embossed
in dulled silver.)

quiet crystals form where my fingers
brush, where my breath fogs—
winter a timid woman
whose small, cold hand
grips mine with the fierceness
of adoration, or fear.

parched streets stretch forth
with a fertile hunger, tongue-wet,
licking my feet. on either side, houses
that dare not speak; windows that dare
not open. moon the silent pendulum
under whose sway
thousands upon thousands
sleep.

but these are my waking hours, when
thoughts are harvested like slender winds,
& the grasses of solitude waver. (stand still.)
sky-fish blink their citrine eyes
in the dark, navigating by sound, & find refuge
in the round hollows of hills. the long shadows
of vanished shapes teeter, precarious
& tender as tight-ropes. (snapped threads.)

each moving thing flickers into being
& then out, in quick succession—ghosts shuffling
past each other surreptitiously, hesitant neighbours,
hushed thieves. moths folded into black triangles.
upon these lines (heavy with indecision,
light with haste), the birds of night gather
in soft bouquets.

seducing a poem

poem with a slim waist, poem that looks good—
that's the thing. come here poppet on little black shoes.
piano shadows across your face:
black white black white black. come here.
you monochrome wonder, why you shine infinitesimal?
you make no sense.
your knee bends easy, in a high ribbed sock of wool.
your hair a scent of question marks.
is this a one-night stand?—one day—one century—
you angling like light, like water over silk.

tiles glisten, bare eyes. here we are. the world's watching.
I'm seducing a poem, working through a whole day
for her—menu, wine, electricity—gentle fan of flowers
for the merest brush of her palm. every little thing. empty
this restaurant of pedestrians, stray poodles of thought—
clean the floor, close the blinds—not too tight,
not to block out all light, but dimmer, more beautiful, so
that bar & counter shine.
golden glass & crystal, wood a gleaming brown.

even my soul polished for her: floor of mind open,
heart waiting, hands clenched so sweet & tight.
wool pockets. tension sparks my nerves—your feet—
little black shoes beyond the door. I move to the table,
behind the slender chair, mouth dry.
your thigh a pale silt glistening. come in, come in.

I look away from the table when you sit down—
I *dare* not look at you—
but there you are, encased in ice, in folded flowers of
light, in the tumbler on the bar.

must move quickly. before you go. I almost ruin it,
in my impatience—your eyes distract me—
your shoes that glint like tears.
must move. move now.

your hand is quiet. yet it's speaking to me
more than you are: it's closer to me, a fog of heat
on the cool of the table. I glance down—up again.
move. move now. but your hand moves first. mine
flinches—surprise? no, not quite—
the poem always makes the first move.
it's ridiculous because no one's watching
& everyone is, & the tiles are people, & I'm trying
to be quiet. ah, fog, heat—your palm so soft & tender.
the whorl of your thumb, minuscule, pressed against my
wrist. my pulse beating in syllables.

you, poem, beautiful. language means nothing.
your words mean nothing—
I can barely hear them—slow slick slide
of tongue in mouth
is all they are.

your mouth. I watch it carefully, winged thing that it is,
I the starved lepidopterist.
the catalogue of your body: elbow, skirt, curve of arm,
shadow of clavicle that dips, a warm boat.
you tender warm thing, I will be careful.
must not hurry—
contrary to hunger, must not—*cannot*—

your foot taps. damn it. blinds threaten to open—

no, wait! I lean across, suddenly urgent, remembering
last time how you opened for me.
must have you. your mouth, winged, tries to fly away.
wait, poem! you're smiling. wait...
I'm leaning across, table a soft chasm: it caves under us
like a bed. the floor melts—
& there it is, your language, your mouth, slow sweet
slide & oh you give me your words.
no crosses of fire here—a gradual spinning of stars,
white threads of light
so gentle in my nerves. your palm shifts
against my wrist—cloth falls—
distant tumbler of heart falling—
my knees waiting on
your sweet floor.

light tilts, glass spilling, blinds opening,
no, not yet, not yet—
I open my mouth to gasp you out, to keep you safe,
to hide you, to kill you, to write you in the air—

—but it's too late. dusk-light, bright orange
& the blinds are open—my own eyes opening.
your glass upended on the table.

swift scent of questions. you're gone.

then

it was then I woke:
it was then I found the hours
of your wrist, green hours
lifted from a passing book,
from an open pocket—
stolen hours.

it was then I woke.
the music of your mouth
now silenced. out where
the light had found us, our
birds were quiet—the branches
of your words still quivering
in the autumn frost.

it was then I woke.
the shallow sky licked clean
of rain, your foot a sharp chill
against mine. out where the light
had found us, our silent steps
now doused by snow. no flame
in your hand or in mine.

it was then I woke.

the night dances

who dances in the bearded garden,
feet slippered in moss?
the night dances, the night dances.

who opens the bed's soft door
& darkens the woodwork with kisses?
the night opens, the night opens.

who blossoms in the small noises
of the dog's beautiful dream?
the night blossoms, the night blossoms.

who gives birth to the poem at sunrise,
after words have taken wing?
the night gives birth, the night gives birth.

who plays the flute of narrow bone
to which you waken, weeping?
the night plays, the night plays.

foreigner, who carries your longing
in the blue urn of twilight?
the night carries, the night carries.

who journeys into the cavern
of the sleeping girl's chest?
the night journeys, the night journeys.

who waits with eyes of yellow smoke
outside the open lighthouse?
the night waits, the night waits.

but most of all, stranger, who lifts
the wing of the dead nightingale
and dances to its song?

the night dances

the night dances.

dismemberment

the stars, spear-tips
upon the night-carved trees.
the hills, knuckled
as the fists of warriors
from a beaten tribe.

the brown boy squats
on the moon & dips
his fingers into the black sea
of night, searching
for his reflection.

& sees
nothing.

these are the Northern Territories,
but the boy knows that this place
is south even of south, south of
hell & south of darkness,
down in the belly of the beast
where none dare wander.

none. no   ne. no   one.
for the boy is no one.
(he has no reflection.)
his mother is no one.
(she cannot see herself in him.)
he was stolen; his mother looks
into another child's face, now,
& dreams him into it.

but dreams can only be dreamt
out of. sleep is for victorious
warriors. not these defeated spirits,
these silent ghosts,
afraid to roam the earth
since the great beast is sleeping.
(they dare not wake it.)
here, insects crawl like lice
among the grass. shadows whisper & touch
each other's empty bodies.

"For we are shadows,"
the boy's grandmother had said.

for we are shadows. all of us.
for when hearts begin to dismember
themselves it is for a greater

cause. some ancient fish rises out of our
bellies & tears out of our barren
wombs. a hydra of conceptual

nothingness, from where we hoist
our blood-soaked flags & smile at the rising
void within.

dichotomy

I recall a time when I used to
prefer silence, but now I know that mercy is
inevitable, like the tide.

       it smothers everything.

             the universe is a smog
of mercies, overlapping & obliterating
each other. a blue pallor (as of dawn)
that thickens into smoke. there's no question
of balance, for if it were to exist, it would surely be

       yellower than this

             more harmonious, more
equitable. there is no justice. only mercy.
your mercy is my hell; my hell is your mercy;
your hell, mine; mine; yours. we push & pull,
children at a park. the dice spin.

       the board comes around.

             in your car are still
the things I had left in it; in your mind,
the words I had spoken. in stars of dust
our daughter finds her hope. there is mercy
in everything.

       if you are bluer now

             than you were then, it is likely
because you are mercy's minion—you, soft-shoed,
walking on my palm. I never did

       grasp you. sleep curls, a quiet lion
outside your door. does it guard you from me?
merciful, indeed. mercy, too, falls in the sound
of our daughter's cough, which rocks
like a broken cup in the night. I walk to her bedroom.

       glimpse her white toes:

chalk smudges. closed flowers.
there was a time you used to curl—
there was a time—
within my door
our daughter's feet like yours.
mercy is inevitable. you, smoke-swift, have come & gone.
the flame remains. the flame
twining in equal parts, our tongues.

sagano

sky a rain-tremble
away from here, thick as the lashes
of Van Gogh's brush, slender
as a given thing, all newspaper & washed ink.
tongue-glitter of dark road
sounds of susurration (silk sleeves over grass)
the wind a tall woman moving through the fields,
hair unbound
& damp.

voices, whispers

such is summer—
voices of gold, whispers of silver—
cloud-edges limned
        in burning white, wind shaping
the grasses with a slow, careful hand:
a mother's hand through
        a child's sun-shorn hair.

leaves stutter forth,
nervous pedestrians
on tall, invisible escalators,
carried up to a great glass ceiling
        blown smooth
by the breath of the sun.

& beneath, as in any crowd,
blue thieves of sound
rustle in tree-corners:
wings folded (hidden pockets),
        beaks tucked
(quiet hands).

bloom

movement, tremble, entirely.
the grace of a hidden moment
wing-glitter of first light
you on the sill,
blossoming
quietly.

answer

the unnamed longing
in your recollection of snow.
I searched with you, don't forget,
for all that you lost. the lone crow
of your memories knows
better than to wait, a distant
speck against the horizon.
I searched the blue cavern
of my skull before I answered
you: *Lonely*, I said. *Iron.*
you pledged your return
on my answer. on fairer
weather. open your hat
of gentle wasps, my dear.
the shapeless threat
of your departure.

painter

night the slurring stranger you meet
moon's pale coin jangling
in his throat, his wide black mouth

painter, here I meet your
apples by the window:
the night in them, glistening,
tired glow of your mind
a quiet lantern lit.

you lover of dusk,
night your only friend.
a lone bird you walk
back & forth, brush feathering
in your hands. the solitude
of your canvas stretched
a white night before you,
what moon what eye

you open onto the east.

sandrock

o crazy bird, what sounds you out?
the waves crash relentlessly,
curled larvae of foam: waves in white
wings of salt. bejewelled birds of the sea.
sounds trapped in small rocks.
o crazy bird, song-like...

terrible the shame of the sky.
overhanging rocks of cloud, faceless:
o bird against the blue, sharp
sickle against the wide curve of glass.
caught on the up-swing: o crazy bird
hurtling into the expanse, fearless.

bird below the wave, wild sea-music
bird over the wind, white-specked.
wings lust-dampened. o crazy bird
of fortitude: everlasting keel, wheel
of sun song-chastened.

too fond

you're too fond of reason to be a poet.
too fond of articles. conjunctions. misused
commas. they find you in public toilets,
playing with your mind, & arrest you
for indecency. oranges & dusk paint
still lifes of you by the sidewalk. abandoned
by your art, your cigarette burns out
in the hole that used to be the moon.

where are you? where are you?
the stones ask. (silence greets them.)
you answer only to the sky, which has
the audacity to imitate the sand's night-glitter.
are you a traffic light, forgotten in your longing
for dawn? are you lost in the vacuum
of love? what emptied you out, what gathered
you in the deep, dark belly of moss?

spit out by the minds of children, poetry
gathers on the pavement. skating rinks
echo the light, their sickled backs sharp
beneath the sun. you squint into the clouds.
perhaps you were holding knives, gently,
in the hand that forgot how to write. in any
case, you've murdered the silence now,
& they'll arrest you again. too late.

two thousand

I went & went,
& the smoke went with me
carrying its smooth parcels
of grief. stomachs tucked
themselves like handkerchiefs.
we weren't hungry. the fires
burned nonchalantly, as if
those weren't our homes,
our footsteps, our bones.
cattle disappeared.
slow hands carried swift guns.
roofs, once thatched, now gaped
like mouths. rain answered them.
I followed the yellow & the grey,
safe colours, colours of clay.
pots broken, ribs carrying water,
wagons quieter than feet. a child's
battered blue skull, cradled
in cotton. a single crow
stealing from an abandoned
hut. I went & went, beyond
our village, beyond our school,
where the ash settled & the roads
emptied, one by one. the wagons
lifted away, like mist. insects
trembled beneath the roadside
leaves. the rain stopped.
the path softened.
the fires were burning, & then
they weren't, but I went & went.
the smoke went with me.

nightchild

phosphorous tumble of
night clouds & you,
dandelion-thin,
moving
over the dim grass.

when the storm hit
the sky fell, as if
carrying you
in its belly—
night-child, why do you
weep, why do you
never weep?

virgin curve of your ankle
soft dust of your skin:
your lilac tongue that never
speaks. night-child, my child,
why do you
run from me?

familiar

in the dark, to know
the shape of things,
to know where they are—
there is no greater mercy.
a bright-lit room
is less comforting
than a darkness
whose contours
are familiar.

gilt trip

gilt curtains, gilt tassels,
sash of your skirt
o quiet bird, tree-still are you
against the sky
as if pinned to it,
breath held (never released)
grey as a stone & silent as one
yet bright, rain-bright & gold
all tassel & hand & backward glance
your throat, your mouth, your ear
o quiet bird, dark-lit are you
as if from within,
when you are caught
you will never sing.

sister

the round ankle of the sun
gleams by the pale tree
that is your corpse. don't tell me,
sister. don't speak of the truth
that everyone knows. the wheel
rolls over your coffin, gentle
as a wave, gentle as the rise
of the hill behind your house.
your chimney's black mouth
now silenced. where do you
wait, with the trembling white
leaves of your feet? where
do the children of your hands
gather? by the stove, little
stones with your name carved
on them. I wait on the doorstep
for your footfall, the empty cradle
of your arms. in the shed I find
you with your sewing machine,
the blue cloth of forgetfulness
under your fingers, the birds
of your thoughts still perched
on the quiet shelves.

turandot

my palms green with shavings of hospital paint.
& still you say: *I'll wait.* oh, really? what for?
chipping away, layer by layer, at the skin of these walls—
for even walls have skins—eyes—ears. our gods in tiny
red parcels. gold cloth. you bring them to me,
unwrap them, as if they were parcels of food.
gods for the devouring. I pity them.
their wide eyes, black-rimmed, fixed forever
as if in death. their eternal ferocity. their paw-like hands
carved into their abdomens. fingers twined. meditating,
of course. are they calm? are they at the centre
of their universe? my schizophrenia, you say, is a lack of
faith. if only I were to gather myself. grains of rice.
my mind is starved. my faith, a perforated stomach. come
back to us, you say. *why do you live in fear?* why, indeed?
good question. psychosis is such a pale

        gift.

     forever
    unraveled.

christmas for non-christians. the horror of a stolen past.
when you unwrap our gods for me, your hands warm
& not-quite-trembling—when you unwrap them,
you open a maw of despair, not unlike blue glass,
in my mouth. I speak, but only marbles emerge.
my words roll uselessly across the floor.
we watch them together. the gods watch them.
they are the gods, I say. *my words.* you don't
believe me.

     who believes
   a thief? not I.

thought-stealer. your own thoughts, spidery with hope,
crawl about & about the truth. there is a truth.

you believe that. who is
this soothsayer you trust? you leave the gods for me—
to listen to, you say. but I have enough to listen to.
don't you know, sister?
when you're gone, I play with our gods
as if they were dolls. they're so gentle in my hands.
not cruel at all. even the fierce trident-holder
does nothing more than prick my fingers. the goddess
of song remains stubbornly silent.
are the gods deaf to me? no. I'm deaf.
selective hearing is the privilege of the new. over time,
all voices converge, into this great teeming river
                    salmon
                            kind nightmares
        froth.
disconnected always. the radio doesn't work.
then again, I *am* the radio. long antennae extended.
when you touch them
with your believer's palms, perhaps
a bit of your belief
        will transfer to me.
does confinement work, as a form of therapy?
of course. the city's infested with fleas. it's a stray
I'd rather stay away from. rabies. causes madness,
you know. my disbelief is no more criminal than yours.
you don't believe me. I don't believe your gods.
our gods, you say. you're right.
the embroidered battle-axe
may be silken to the touch, but surely, its blade
slaughters souls. your god-doll in my hand. a strange
reverse voodoo. with time, you will visit me less & less.
I know this. you too will abandon me, sister. like

our gods. the elephant head, the lotus feet,
the never-ending chatter of love. for gods talk
                    in the language
                        of love. it is
vast & terrifying. their love is as indifferent
as light. falling upon everything, baring everything.
merciless.
& you ask me why I'm afraid. when I talk to them, only
a piercing silence
greets my voice. they are indifferent. I am indifferent.
my worship
your hand
  our cloth.
skin bound & unbound. the walls coalesce.
your gifts, our gods, my commonplace.
this playground, paint shavings stain my feet, not grass.
sister, will you not play with me? you'll be gone soon,
as they say. last phantom, last riddle, last curse.
you & your slippers. your gods
wandering footless. leave me your little dolls. so precious
to me, your vocabulary of storms. unshakeable faith.
blue marbles. I wrap & unwrap our gods for you.
won't you come back to us?
you speak from the walls. every echo of your call
sheds more green shavings. they fall at my feet, soft moss.
silence, shaped by agony, becomes smooth. like a flute.
our blue-skinned god plays a tune on it. the eternal
            disappears, a magicked
      glove. perhaps you were
the goddess of song. but you won't
        any longer.
          visit
me.

spires

gentle universes that float past
like tall, starry ships
the guard at the dark door & the booted
heel, beloved, do you hear it
our bars made silver spires by night

hunger

my children at the cemetery of violins.
dark wood arching above their heads,
their pouch-like stomachs empty
of song. hunger tastes sweet
to those who've forgotten fullness.

my children with blue legs
behind the small hive of thoughts.
each buzz illumined in the night,
a small glow of hunger in the large
dark belly of the violin.

my children crouched on river
banks. silt feeding their mouths,
the warm and the wet of it gathered
in their fists. the white lotus of each hand
cupped in the river of memory.

the butterflies of hunger are few.
my children hunt them in the red
forest, where flowers of green
become pale eyes. violins curve
their dark smiles on the trees.

tavern

you enter unannounced,
soothsaying bird on your shoulder—
where from, wanderer?
the honeysuckle glitter of your hair
the quiet castanets of your feet
your breath speaking the language
of silence. they've grown fond
of it, silence their ally,
silence their beloved foe,
each word of it familiar to them
as you are to the wind.
the curve of your instep
an insult to speech: the tilt
of your chin the pause
that breaks their pity. you give
it back to them tenfold. soothsayer!
the violet string of light
curled around your feet
lets you escape. uncharted still
the seas of you, the white shores
of your arms, the birds of your
hands. each wing a word
unplucked, adrift. for me,
soothsayer, leave a feather
behind.

visitor to ward 9

woman shaped like a vase
(head, flowers, arm)
& the man, drawing portraits
on vinyl. on air scratched
with dust, odd streaks of light
are made transparent marble:
air giving up, giving shape,
conforming to vase
& water & the unbearable
heaviness of skin.
she wears her legs:
cloth-puppets, filled stockings,
stitches coming loose
as he washes them. gentle,
gentle, for there is no
chart at the foot of her bed
no music, no heart—
gentle, gentle, curve of bone
& light, as they dance
on the scratched-vinyl floor.
(im)mortal & contained
they drink from each other,
as if the truth hadn't spilled,
sand-like, from the spout.

glass

dawn breaking its bread:
oh the flat earth, the empty plate
the shining rim, & the sea
dropping upon it like a slow mouth,
a silver tongue, hot & sun-shorn
& achingly smooth, jagged within
like the human soul but so smooth,
so smooth, bird in perfect parabolic curve
above a glass desert, suspended
as if by thirst.

sunrise

truth is, no rhyme can save me
but you wouldn't hear me admit to that
no, not in polite company.

the void, in silken stockings,
exits
stage left.

night curls itself around my finger.
o violin of a woman's back,
pale breath of dawn—

grass, green whisper that it is,
kisses my shoes. the sky bends
its blistered back. the amiable torture
of a quiet sun

& I beneath it
flowering
like fresh blood.

ode to ruffles

the ruffles of a marriage bed
& of a child's skirt
& of a midnight playground's
peculiar blue dust—
ruffles come in whispers,
ruffles come softly, loudly,
in drops molten gold
& stubborn. the skin
ruffles over hangnails
& shoulders, & mouths
ruffle, & words through
water. time ruffles in stiff
waves of orange. clocks
stop. start again. a train
ruffles the tracks, heat
ruffles the air, the mother
ruffles her daughter's hair,
a whistle ruffles
the monk's quiet mind.
a newspaper ruffles
with the blackish rust
of an old bruise. the shop's
chime ruffles each god-like
jar, the rounded glass backs,
traffic candy, sealed lips.
a sail ruffles the shark's
smooth white back.
the sea ruffles under the sun.
a ruffled brow, bright light,
the toothless gentility
of a womb. ruffles congeal

in blood banks, on street corners,
in slow twists of sound
through a subway pipe.
ruffles ruffle themselves.
taffeta & musk. corrugated iron.
honey ruffled by gradual hands.
the powdered ruffle of a judge's
wig. of a baby's bottom. ruffles
inhabit. ruffles take over. ruffles
are. ruffles in the gleam
of canned tuna, baked beans,
ruffles in the sneaker's sexual
squeak against the toilet floor,
ruffles in the mirror & even
in its cracks, ruffles in the lipstick,
on the lips, in the tongue, in
the speech, ruffles in the thought
& in the cashew-smooth
curlicues of brain—ruffles within
& without, ruffles in plucked
thread & wrinkled leaves,
money, palms. ruffles forgive.
ruffles never surrender.
ruffles wait, with the authority
of substance, tactile &
ever-giving. ruffles in space.
stars ruffle the lake.
feet ruffle the tarmac,
the lone bulb ruffles its shadow,
the wind-moth ruffles itself,
the cat ruffles its garbage.
a woman's thigh, love-ruffled,
& the night, ruffling a dark
gauze of berries against

the window. the door that
ruffles inwards. the lung
that opens. the ruffling
of breath, the infinite pillow,
the shallow oyster. ruffles
in the finger & on the thumb.
ruffles again on our inner
steps. the basement's
ruffled silence. wooden locks
that ruffle in their solitude.
the ruffle that thrills wool,
that preserves the past,
that carries forth. the ruffle
of a bee's back & of a spider's
legs. a velvet purr of a ruffle.
the ruffle you bring to me,
encased in stone cloth.
the ruffle of a pearl.
the ruffle that brings us
together, with the startled
redness of cloves. the ruffle
that kisses & moves away.
the ruffle that never stops.
the ruffle that separates.

friend

you should know better
than to war with me,
friend. in our fights,
we toss our ships
in memory of old storms—
familiar anchors are cast,
your face the sea,
my word the deep triangular
spear, black-arrowed,
smooth-backed. from where
you sit, so far away,
you manage to halt
the sun in its fury,
motionless & smothered
above the dead waves.

what lone bird?
what supplication?

there is a smoothness
to our enmity. as of
a relic. perhaps it is
even precious to us,
shaped by both our hands,
a composition of caves,
twin darknesses.

the sorrow of textures:
the weight, the shadow.

your feet, my soil.
your fire, my clay.

aubade at city diner

implacable, impervious summer:
no sun of york to blossom here, with
doped-up eyes & fearless heat. scraping by
on the occasional high—gutter-funk music,
love in bonsai trees. little cars that pass
for excuses. hunting in the forest
of the sprawling city, deer-quick eyes
& sleight-of-hand: amphetamines, gentle
pockets of bliss, white flowers of ants.
euphoria. the tarmac a swaying bridge,
a cliff one leap away from flight.

old lady sings jazz in the pre-dawn chill,
summer in her smoothened voice.
smoke gathered in black blossoms:
summer folded in a gleaming cloth
of mist over the cars. sea-scent from
the pier, heavy as the weightless rain.
the jazz lady falls silent. summer
dope-sweetened, implacable
as the trees of love. blood-music
in the city's blue breath. the sun
at the pier, turning in its sleep.

wander

what would you like to do?
what would you like to do?
to wander & wander & never reach.
wander beneath
the stupidly star-pinned sky, high tent
wind unremarked upon
swift flowers
the light like blue hay.
oh, how cruelly lit are you.
wander there
& back again.

silent as the eyes of wolves
wet as cobblestones
& the slow smoke of thought:
mist, hunger, memory
grass-scent & skin.
beloved prey,
what wanderlust are you
what gentle ankle
what eternal walk?
night paint-smudged
beneath your feet.
wander there
& back again.

rehabilitation

the long abyss:
so slender, so solitary.
dawn's pale fruit ripens
in your mouth.

preferring the calm of despair
to the excitement of grief—
was that what you said?
long abyss, indeed.

where did your ship sail,
its white tongue raised
in mockery against the waves?
you who were so indignant,
pared down to the bones
of your thoughts.
I pick at them distractedly.

are the walls clean, where you are?
amphetamine in little pockets.
latitude & longitude,
untruths mapped in marble inches.
your ink on my palm, my skin
still warm. but you've left, now.
taken your shadow, too.

your letters do find me
in good health. my abyss
is brighter than yours, & thinner,
a knife's edge
sparkling with cocaine.

I remember to wash my hands.
I remember to sleep.
sunset's bright orange
still startles me, bringing out
the dark veins of trees
for a fresh blood-letting.
closed eyes. silhouettes.
cars in molten drops of steel
clinging to the tarmac.

no distant road, here.
everything too near.

you needn't worry, wind-sailor.
the birds become the waves,
blue-winged. or perhaps it is the ocean
itself that takes flight, on spumed feathers,
to perch on the fading light.

dawn, noon, dusk, night.
four pieces on the board.
bishop to E6.

another day gone.
another page, you'd say.
no words written.

when will I write back to you?

when the sea is emptied.

but you needn't worry. neatly watched
& pocketed as I am, they take
good care of me. I scavenge their smiles.
your memories.

purification. my slate being
so carefully erased. will your name
be gone, too? the lights of your shore
blinking out, one by one.

a long abyss.

but the walls are clean.

haiku #1: crystal

the crystal throat of
a morning bird, carrying
the wine of the sun.

rose

the fevered rose
opens its shop on our street.
you enter, because the clocks
in its window are divine.
later you tell me, over dinner,
about the rose's thighs. red
as the hour of sunset, you say.
red as the hour of fury. you've
never been so animated.
time doesn't pass in that shop,
you say. the carpet swallows
your memories. you paid
the rose with them, your
grey memories of youth,
your unwelcome memories,
locked away in the black
cabinet at the counter. it
glistens like a jewel, you say.
that cabinet. the rose.
the rose, you say, the rose.
& again, later that night,
you forget my name.

mayur
Trans. "Peacock" in Hindi.

you, who possess
the cut-glass throat
of a green bird—
do you resent
the truth
of your song?

white pebbles,
the gathered dress,
the offered hand—
your feet, softer
even than the soil.
do you resent
the silence
of your footfall?

no forest quietens
for you. no tree bends
its quivering ear.
the moon, with its
taste of blue pewter,
ignores your call.
do you, purveyor
of silver things,
resent your
strangeness?

your hands,
wooden with sound,
reverberate with
the memory of
lightning. still burned,
your mind echoes
forgotten voices.
do you, who possess
the patient agony
of a god's ear,
resent your
never-ending
wait?

ghat

to you, language is
the terror of signs:
the curl of a wet ear,
a wagon of shadows,
voiceless passengers.

when you descend
the clay steps
of the temple's *ghat*,
your palms cupped in
supplication, it isn't
the rage of silence
you want, nor
the vertigo of prayer,
but a certain hollow
sound, the rain-slick
repetition of stones,
relentless. each
pebble, each word
cast into the water
is a sacrifice of doves—
the cruelty of a dove,
its white absoluteness.

it is neither wisdom
you want, nor noise,
nor surrender. the stiff
vehicle of your mind
wouldn't permit it, no,
not that. in the thin
blue alleys of yearning,

you ladle out water
as if to quench yourself—
the dim fire of lust,
vermilion within
the wrought cage.

what is it you seek?
to forget or to regain
yourself? even the gods
covet the moist corners
of your tongue, where
speech lies dormant,
with its attendant
baggage of lies.

a sweet reconnaissance.
each step into the *ghat*
takes you closer to it,
to your beloved terror,
to the carnivorous fish
that wait, gold-finned,
in the quiet. yet still
you descend, a ripple
of substance into
the belly of a vacuum,
stubborn & desperately
fearless, like dust.
your feet, your ankles,
your calves, your thighs—
a ballooning of bright
cloth around your waist,
swollen as a lotus root.

you extinguish
your palms against
the sky-mirror; they quiver,
doused wicks. perhaps
you are a coward,
or a tree, your descent
unmarked even by
the sun. here you
will stay, as the hours
pass, undressing
skin by skin, petal
by petal. by the end
of it, there may be
nothing left of you
but a single nerve,
a beaten track
of dull metal,
a pulsing husk.

this is what you seek:
even though death
resides in the shallows,
even though the moths
of old thoughts settle,
in hushed lines, along
the dawn's pale
shoulders. you wash
your eyes, your ears,
your brow, again
& again, until the water
burns your features
into facelessness.

the erasure of signs.
when it comes, at long
last, you know. this
is what you seek:
the soft iron of mouths,
the infinitely slow
drift of a large bird,
the heavy kiss of
clouds, smothering
everything.

haiku #2: glimmer

stars, dull stones, glimmer
under the dark water of night.
white lotus of moon.

the woman & death

white spider, what an arch
of sugar your throat is!
listen to the words you speak!
music! the blue griffin of your back
opens its beak against your
neck. the spread wings of your
arms, wavering at the cliff's edge,
the bright sun of your forehead
extinguished by the rough wind.
what death you carry in your
narrow voice! mnemosyne!
your name a drop of forgetfulness.
quench my thirst for me,
moth-keeper. the broken urn
of your mouth, glistening
with the ashes of yesterday,
still holds my thirst.

vigil

whalers with gentle eyes
swab the red off their decks.
you of the night, black as the night,
glistening—I watch your large flanks
heave, curling my toes
into the wet wood.

laughter and *sake*. my cup
so small. where is your truth, gone
because I asked, because
you said so? your tongue
as rich as loam, soft beneath
the old sheen of your eyes.

talk to me like the others do.
open your belly to the night
that is yourself. answer
my question. I'll wait
with aching haunches
while the sun-shadowed wind
dries the deck beneath my feet.

stone

curious flowers open their mouths,
bird-like. the stone's infinite shadow
unfurls its black tongue.

what chair of cloud
graces the heavens?

the office of bliss unoccupied.

o silent stone, river-quiet
clothed by a single leaf.
o tidy stone, round crystal
a glittering spark of heat.

the sky quietens, for the stone
speaks. rain gathers in startled
bouquets. little stone, bird of the earth,
song of the earth. the tall grasses
bend their ears.

what music finds the curved
horns of dust?

open the dark cupboard of words.

fruit borne in the stone's blue
silence. the wind, slow-footed,
lulling itself to sleep...

dowry

she carries her thighs
to the service station:
a rain-daughter's
dowry.

they wait for her
with veils of parchment:
translated letters,
petrol fumes,
burnt paper.

this wasn't
part of the bargain,
she says.

but it was,
the clouds reply.
it was.

proselyte

an exhausted mind finds cars
meaningless. ridiculous can-openers
pry open the teeth of night. the city
waits on ruddy haunches, embarrassed
by the mind that sleeps within it:
the mind that wakes when the last
rose has wilted, that staggers
along the sidewalk, sleep-talking
of blue conspiracies, of presidents
crowned upon this lowly isle.
asphalt in glittering waves.
exhaustion that wavers weapon-like:
mornings in the dream-ripple,
nights in the quiet wallet.
the street opens its shallow mouth
to unsuspecting veterans.
convert of the city, exhaustion:
the siren song of memory.

haiku #3: violets

blue somnambulists
roam the fields: night-violets
rustled by the wind.

cherub

broken terrace of cloud
on which your feet shimmer.
sky-child, death-child,
your eyes always closed
to the sun's violet flower—
where is your mother? where
do her feet, white-shrouded,
wander? her soft arms of air
a cradle you've forgotten.

the yellow window of lust
you open onto the world:
all things bright to your
glimmering eyes, your
open tongue. the silence
of your mouth, the clear winter
of your mind, both ringing
with the sound of passing light—
by the running river of desire
I find you shoeless, bathing.

poetics of solitude

poem: the long dance around a thing,
as close to it as possible, without touching it.
proximity of self unbearable. limited fool.
where did the burning go? lone body of the moon,
dust-laden, hidden in the folds of night.
the poem unashamed. nude leaves of thought.
tiny syllables march: even the boat now emptied,
still as the water's thin feet. words by their lonesome.
the deep candle lit. never the gentle speaker sleeps.
harvest of dreams, straitjacket fever. the courage to be
senseless. waves of silence that crash against
the mind's blue shore. distant the reach of the visible.
forever in an iron spoon. the fence unbroken.
oh where do you wait? alone the poem, forgotten
the poem, the six tongues of music silent. street-lights
in bright helmet fugue. the word unopened.
knees of night, the quiet hair of the moon.
poem: the long dance around a thing...

kirsome

I happen upon a girl shedding skin
a young snake, bathing suit
wound about her ankles. giggles.
the sea's glass shoulder
sloping gently downwards:
dependable, trecherous,
silver-tongued. how easily
she trusts in it. a cool swallow
tenuous as smoke. smothering.
hands on knees, I watch
the bright candle of her hair
disappear, only to emerge
helmet-flat and shining
an instant later. her palms
slap the waves, chastening.
gulls cock their heads;
sand rests in undisturbed
mounds. the sea's loose fist
can't hold her. she escapes.

departure

the old diamond of dawn
glistens by your elbow. let me be
the wolf on your rug, tail thumping,
ears cocked to your every
movement. the slow dance
of goodbye weaves its way
between us, gingerly
as an uninvited guest.
lifted upon the stiff wind
the leaves of tomorrow scatter,
ant-like, in busy millions.

but you'll be going tomorrow
the airport waits with folded wings.
your fingers at your knees, tapping,
the script of departure
curling through your thoughts,
your forehead. my wolf waits
by your feet, ever-loyal,
ever-hungry. they announce
your flight. your eyes leave the sky:
it darkens. the sun's lamp doused
by the retreating wave of your mind.

blue crosses mark the junctures
of your wrists. veins. destinations.
I found no great treasure in you,
save the long silence of common
loss, the dim light of love extinguished.

may you find your empires still. leave
me the pearl of memory, harvested
from the deep, damp caverns of
your past: belated, exquisite,
half-formed. you're leaving now,
but I, with my wings of ash, have left

already.

kingfishers

you sat outside sleep's black door
with your knees drawn up,
the kingfishers of your hands silent.
your dream's blue fronds
stood at alert. nothing moved.
small rats curled by your feet,
awake but quiet, your palm
the warm roof above their furred
backs. the field of nails blossomed
around you. you sat so still,
unmoving, unloving. what dream
stirred in the deep grasses
of your mind?

pale green

Here in the rainy season
I catalogue our differences:

Mao's still face,
a bike's seat collecting water
the warm bone of a woman's hip
dumplings unwrapped,
soft as a baby's skin
steam rising
a white dragon's breath
fogging the windows

Each taste
so incomplete, too complete
this quiet lostness
this still green tea,
its total silence
in the midst of traffic

Ceramic-hot fingers uncurl
a child's leaf-thin hand
creased with labour, with sweat
sweet with the joy
of a fistful of string

Mother says
Mother says
that which is string
in your hand today
is a kite in the sky
tomorrow.
Tomorrow...

boat in echuca

morning in the boathouse
& we're having one of our
ridiculous conversations
again. the lake around us
is composed entirely
of clock hands. their ticking
follows us into our skulls,
watches us through our
eyes, the curved spoons
of our words. your green
purse glitters like a crocodile's
mouth, snaps shut—hush,
hush, listen. out there
the moth of answers
flicks its quiet wings.

city verge

I

this cruel god
the savage green lake
awaits. city's tall towers
glass-water of each window.
his horns do multiply
beautifully, this god
in smoke incarnate, the city's
cars in trembling traffic. bent backs
of steel still glittering. where
I stood with feet suspended
fifteen storeys oh fifteen storeys
above the ground, sound
filtered through floors of smoke,
god speaking to my lonely
ear. the grass stretches,
lake-like. my green feet ripple
beneath the skyscrapers.
heat rises like water. god
in every decibel, every broken
syllable, the unborn baby
& the politician still wrapped
in crumpled headlines. ions for
dessert. the dirty floor of
carbon (die) oxide:
so still the water of truth.
my city in glass slippers.

II

the lake stood, a tall flower
in the midst of our city.
cars blossomed carelessly,
hidden bees of smoke
buzzing, fused infrastructure,
violent ants. the red of each
shoe forgotten. children with
traffic lights for faces. oh
forgetfulness. the city on its
last legs. water in every street:
river, tributary. the lake must
end by lunch-time. off
until 2, the sky, lamp-lit
lighting our summer tree.
cars with hooded eyes.
wooden smoke lost
in blind buildings, seeking
an exit, windows shut
with the finality of traps.
the lake of noise
no longer green.
this opera never-ending.
the slow scream of opened
rivers, roads, hot tarmac
& watered cars. fish-tanks,
street pumps, the still lakes
of junkie eyes. glass biscuits.

III

no god doesn't know oh
traffic by the blue scimitar.
the anger of prayer, true silence.
the city in woken birds. wings of
smoke folded at the precipice.
nothing crueler than this.
construction workers buying
pet roaches for their daughters.
see the little pouches of women
standing at alert. traffic yellow:
the long wilderness of a street.
taxis in broken circles. the small
waist of a forgotten road. lakes
still wait in fire-lit darkness,
blue offices, the black corners
of folded moths. the quiet wasp
of water at the tunnel's damp
mouth. last overture
of the lake, glass isles.
traffic forgotten in lost indices.
cars hunched over, children
perched like gazelles.
the sidewalk treacherous.
smoke, the gentle noose
around our city's neck. bruised
the soft night & the slow dawn.
ruddy face lit. white traffic lights.

pyre

my father in a pale cowl, hooded,
watching. in the air a lovely ash
that shone like little smiles.

my feet in shoes of flames,
wind-carried, this warmth a satin dress
eating me up. this quiver-quiet,
this surrender.

& beyond it, the sky's soft mouth.
such a red patience. a very sweet answer
in the opening of this flower.

my father's silence
the music of absence
the sky's mouth closing

over.

petal

you wake up red,
in the curious half-light
of the whirring fan,
each one of your limbs
a petal unfurling.

carnivorous flower,
where are your thoughts?

your thigh, your foot,
your sloping jaw
are all butterflies
gathered in my palm.

where will you fly to,
pale-shadowed thing?

the curve of your back
soft as a white
moth's wing.

bear

today's newspaper reclines
in the chair next to yours,
quiet. I don't dare
reach out to touch you:
your disgruntled paw
on the kitchen table,
curled inwards, harmless.

grief marks its strange
crop-circles in your mind,
your eyes, your long mouth
in which your tongue
lies silent.

don't you remember
the wild caves I saved you from?
I keep your children
in little shelves, in jugs,
& and feed them to you
in milk-warm sips.

don't you remember
the seasons? our spring,
our forest of flowering noise
for which you fought
nail and tooth, soothsayer.

forget

one can forget
how to write a poem:
the awkwardness of time
spent away from a lover,
love-letter, littering
love on the pavement
generously. who left
these leaves for me?

I alone know the numbers
of these red-brown things,
thin letters the wind
has left to me, paint
in dappled grey along
the walls, the sidewalk,
your shadow.

at the place I waited
for you the numbers
still linger, the dates,
hanging on twigs.
so delicate the dance of this
forgetfulness.

tell me, wind,
the words you kissed
onto the pavement, the leaf-wet
mouth you pressed to me.

a long, long dance
has passed me by. open
your answers. wait for me.

list of replicates

where go the french?
death in shallow spoons.
found: item 1, the breasts of cloud,
scorn-softened. the caregiver
of rain still silent, shadowed
by the stubborn roof. item 2,
a bottle of lethe. forgetting
the music of moss. the trees
still standing, wind-bowed,
their feet scarred by fire.
item 3: the thunder
of silence. replicate love,
quotients of loss. the foreigner
at the cliff, waiting. item 4:
one strand of hair, curled.
poison in a note of music.
the harbour of belated vows,
the ship of past departures.
item 5: the house, listless.
where you dropped
your cigarette, the carpet
still singed. the dust of
your thoughts clinging
to the curtains. item 6:
two brown shoes, rain-wet.
the blood of your prey
pooled under the lamplight.
your claws retracted.
item 7: a dictionary of french.
a cave of words, dark-bound.

red spines of love. your flight
that left on tuesday. stubborn
lies. the stain of old frowns.
item 8: one syllable, formless.
the bottle spilled. the question
unanswered. the last day
of the week, your continued
silence.

b(i)rth

there is nothing familiar
in this dream
save a timorous spine
& my mother's hands,
chattering with bangles,
fingers folded
like wings.

these hollow bones
sang the song of my blood,
her blood, an opening cavern
of mouth & womb
that I remember
not remembering.

where is the centre of it,
the gravity of this
flowered being
that walks on two feet
but recognises not itself?
what am I giving birth to
in this memory of myself?

in the pulse of it
there is a code
of numbers written
in black blood-sand:
sifting away from the shores
of her skin, getting lost
in the wave
of each heartbeat,
each crash.

creating a life
isn't difficult when
it half-creates itself,
insistent, stubborn
beyond all reason
& effervescent.
a small glow,
oyster-soft, within
this folded shell.

sweatshop blues

daddy-o on the long boat
daddy with the sail-shaped triangle
of a shark: my daddy, the pet of moths
my daddy never-ending, his blue pocket
of insolence lost, my daddy lonesome,
in rose compressed

daddy da-dum da-dum
daddy in a soft tin drum
beating out the blood of a song
my daddy in dark feet, red sand
my daddy in straitjacket fugue
daddy in the slow-rising sap of dawn

daddy's note pressed between
the leaves of my mind. daddy's trough
of union men: daddy mining the deep abyss,
daddy singing the sweatshop blues.
drowned in the smoke of the chimney-hat
daddy stepping over the threshold of death...

burn

he keeps the quiet things
indoors. flowers, maps,
memories, the skin of his mind
smooth as a new burn
& tender. *don't wake me up,*
he says to the smiling walls,
the blackened floor.

outside, noise rages
& he flinches at it,
but in here it's cool,
so dust-laden & silent,
the dim light a thin blanket
of warmth across his shoulders.

there's old ink in the lines
of his palm, in his veins.
he's a written word
curled in on itself.
fading. *don't leave me,*
he says to his house.
don't leave me.

seaworthy

life's an extenuating
circumstance. you make
excuses, excuses, kind sounds
tripping up your ears. in your
hand a box of clues, you walk
around with it, maybe
this cigarette will light
itself like women do,
incandescent. & then
you'll know. in the mean time
(for time's never kind)
you find yourself a car
a lovely transport, a little
star on wheels, spinning.
you used to have these
orange tops—they spun
like that back in the day.
teaspoons measured in
oceanfuls. boat engines,
whale bellies scoured with
soap. don't mope. life's clean
when you want it to be.
(or not.) your surgeon
scrubs his hands at any rate:
your fate guides you to him,
to this white sea of walls.
within the silent gasp of air
you can hear your
heart ticking. that box
of clues still cradled in
your palm, still unopened,

so tight & dear its corners.
it's like a family heirloom.
indestructible. precious.
there's a reason you didn't
open it. the flame is out,
the top's spinning, air
thinning. this star a little
car, a little boat engine
churning. excuses, excuses,
dear teaspoon. your mouth's
an oceanful. antiseptic blue
marbles, kind clicking sounds.
a whale's clean tongue
that speaks the password.
the box is open.
your engine's gone.

the sun still rises

this woman a cutlass.
curious the black cave of night.
where did I come from?
where do you go to?
earth a revolving mirror.
sand in buried spades.
class, poverty, race,
sex measured in cupfuls.
when did we run out of rice?
dry water, your hair curlers
left by the broken dresser.
my feet bare on the torn mat.
your eyes find your hands.
they curl, lonely earthenware.
trees in solitary laughter.
why do you wait? inside
the trembling moth my tongue.
I was silenced by the war.
the rich gun you carry.
the dark oil-fever. your
forehead warm, my hand
seeking your sun-hot skin.
the temple of mind behind your
eyes. touch me when you can.
it's a family plan. our children
quiet in the ghetto of song.
our terrible hut silent.
the roof of thatched air.
knotted knees against the dirt.
oh open your mouth:

the tanker full. water brown
from our pump. you drink it,
I drink it. the oil-fever sets. over
the dry heart of our land,
our children bent like sickles.
our hunger sings
through the whip-thin trees.
the wind of drought retreats.
the sun still rises.

bushwalk

the blue whisper of tyres
the road bending under our knees.
we lifted above, kites of lonely mind.
patches of green beneath us.
out here the clouds bird-like,
the silence of the sun, the tall
caverns of leaves. o tundra of
forgotten trees. the heel of earth
escapes, dust rising. water bends
over the rise of land. we wait,
flasks in hand, mouths drinking.
truth: the song of quiet things.
we leave the earth as we found it,
unchanged, but the earth
leaves us: discovered.

shape-shifter's song

the pale apple of the girl's hand.
the diver finding the pearl of his own eye.
narrative peace in the untold story.
the painter's soul under the autumn tree.
merciless the symmetry of the flower.
the blue ink of smoke unfurling in the sky.
old watches on the ebony dresser.
the woman on the deserted path.
black rubies of the night.
wild grasses of the abyss.
the broken wheel, translucent.
the cloak of wind, sun-warmed.
the careful rain of winter.
the open window at dawn.

sundress

the sun's blue hat wavering
at the cliff's edge. the girl's hand
that reaches out to catch it.
o music of the sun, where
do you wander? torn lace
of cloud gathered in a dress
of froth: sweet the bloom
of this foreign skirt.

knees of earth browned
beneath the fists of trees.
grass in alert handfuls.
the painter on the lone hill,
brush in hand. the girl in
her sundress, blossoming.
the lake, a blue glitter of
silk-warmed sun. never-ending
the broken cup of sky.

exodus

careless the bend of the physical.
why do you wait? cherubs in lonely
splashes of pink wait by the sidewalk.
angry urchins of flowers. pockets
unfurl themselves in the drunken
breeze. out here, poetry lives
in the artist's hungry shoes.
thoughts gather frost by charred
windows. anthems of deserted
bliss roam the highways.
the poem loses weight, the poet
slams the door as he leaves.
traffic lights wait, dew-draped,
for dawn. truths gather in
glittering puzzles of asphalt.
eyes watch from the corner store,
unblinking. cigarettes bloom in black
flowers by the skating rinks. torn jeans
speak their poetry to the dust.
o traffic lights, why do you wait?

taxonomy

& *she*, that doesn't know
an ounce of honest suffering—

suffering makes one honest,
does it?

I only mean—
suffering gives one texture.

texture.

I knew you'd say that.

she's not a bloody piece of cloth.
texture. like she's some—

bats in the belfry. bats...

a human being is only honest
when she suffers.

suffering. a candle burning
at both ends. reading a book
in the dark. sequins.
the glitter of eyes.

I grew familiar with my mask.

suffering—shells—masks—

suffering made me intimate
with my mask.

suffering stripped me
of my mask.

loud ribbons cast ashore.
the sea in whispers.

I heard she suffered deeply.

depth. suffering gives one depth.

the abyss of stars looks on, faceless.

there's no depth in darkness.
all things are a surface. one surface.
blindness...

stringing beads of memory. suffering
in the tracks of a needle. speed, honey, ice.
mice in the clockwork.

bats in the belfry. I said...

suffering is hunger. hunger is

but I

but it

hunger is

hunger is

small pillows of thought. hunger
in puddles. so easy to lose the leash.
I held it a while ago...
suffering. suffering is the leash.
suffering is the throat.

parallel universes float past, oblivious
as fish. their tall fins pass by,
ghost ships.

oblivious... suffering is oblivious.

sequins sew themselves into
pillows of eyes. they watch in the dark.

surfaces merge. replicate themselves.
faces reflected in concave curves.

the never-ending hunger
of a spoon.

eternity in neat bites.

suffering is hunger is oblivious is

thoughts peck at each other,
cantankerous as crows.

did she suffer much?

much. few. many. long.

suffering is relative.

suffering is absolute.

in the sand they wrote her name.
the sea, stubborn as always,
refused to wash it out.

suffering is stubborn. as a stain.

the stain of old blood, the stink of it;
used tampons in the trash. suffering
is oddly existential. is built of bright
little blocks.

the claws of night beside
my bed. suffering waits.
I wear a blue dress. I wear...

wings are thin by nature. I heard
she suffered only briefly before the end.

brief. causative. caustic. suffering is.

threads unravel themselves
they sew sequins into her skin.

she suffered gently.

like a tree.

are trees gentle?

is suffering gentle?

I don't mean to be aggressive. defensive.
I don't mean—

I don't.

by the voices the light is near.
the light is near by the voices.

crows of thought disappear,
one by one. it's so lonely here.

suffering is lonely.

suffering is crowded.

walls of bruised red
cave inwards on all sides.
a ceiling of paper smothers
all breath. air. she needs air.

order in the pack. wolves. cards.
the fur that ran beneath my fingers
ran over her thighs.

I counted her suffering.
it folded obediently
beneath my numbers.

call it, call it now—

suffering is infinite. suffering is limited.

her eyes became sequins
that came away in the wash.
laundry waits for no one.

suffering is impatient.

suffering is patience itself.

self-awareness fades in & out.
I hear things. she says things.
which one of us is mad?

the moon hides behind my knees.
boo. the children of nightmares
are hungry. the always-hunger
of waiting.

a frog nailed to the table, mid-dissection.

suffering is naked.

like a nude, she posed for me,
clad only in truth. no, wait. that wasn't...

silence undresses while we look away.

suffering restores silence to noise.

noise to silence.

the agony of poised toes. the arch
of the foot, so beloved. the strain
of the ankle. breath
at high altitudes.

suffering is vertigo.

suffering hits the ground.

so she didn't suffer much, did she?

a pity. she deserved it.

pilgrim

the beauty of abandoned gloves
rests gently beside your table-lamp.
your glass of wine, pitch-black: your voice
ragged with loss. you walked so long,
you tell me, to find the open road of
tomorrow. snake-like, the scales of asphalt
glittering, it followed you

with the tenaciousness of death.
wild bees lit the sky in a haze of hot fury.
here, the flask of silence broken, you drink
from the night's blue cup. how tired your eyes
as they recall your journey. the companions
that left you, one by one, to walk alone.
your gloves, empty. your hands, curled.

gratitude

how gently their backs break, you think, with
light tied to their shoulders in straws. bending until
their hands can touch
their shoes. something
cracks. you push your finger down & down
& something
cracks.

their mouths open in surprised relief. under their
skin muscle moves in grey-red glimmers, nerves
sprouting thin blue roots, right down to their
toes that curl hotly in imitation
Italian shoes.

you sense something of your
brokenness in
them. so you break them to see how far
you've been broken.

time's gears wind
back. they will never
stand up again, because you've
broken their backs & now
rain will fall
on upturned umbrellas.
& they will sit in red trucks

& be relieved.

politics of the chair

the chair never stops.
money in pink lotuses:
oh time in minutes, the quiet
forests of suburbs.
secrets in bottled pens.
ink windows. eternity in
the pet rat's cage. radioactive
droppings. green politician's
singular speech: rain
silent on the doorstep,
irony in the curled clouds.
interference of radio bliss,
waves in blue static.
houses with shuttered
mouths. hands misplaced
in pockets. oh nirvana
of furniture. wood
ever-lasting. speech
stops where the eye
begins. needles run
in red circles around
the neighbourhood.
children's feet. stockings
in subdued question-marks.
marx? no, thank you.
the capitalism of the chair
unkind. his kind, her kind,
their kind. kind(er)garten
of ice floes. lichen
on the forgotten tree.
the oil pump so solitary.

wherefrom this joy.
caffeine weightless
in the samurai breeze.
strange warriors walking
in the rain. upturned
umbrellas, black tulips.
capitalism of the unnerved
roof. chimney smoking.
furniture in sullen blocks.
the grandmother waits,
impatient by the cigarette
stand. the conspicuous
yellow thief of sunlight,
snaking around the corner
store. bullets wander freely.
arrogant guns. children
by the sidewalk, flowering.
stubborn goes. the winter,
flawless, stays. white
the rooftops under the sun's
true glare. sound in staccato
queues. trains of people
leave, ant-like. slow storms
of silence. feet on the tiles,
triangular. angry eyes stand
by the bus-stop. drivers
on never-ending strikes.
lightning gentle against
the frothed lip of cloud.
oh furniture, where dost
thou go? the chair
never stops.

the visit

leave the petals here, by the sill.
I want to watch them rise & drift
when the wind breathes upon them.
petals shaped like little boats, but all
they can do is drift.

such a brief visit of yours—while the sky
darkens, you leave a bunch of flowers
by the sill. a bunch of flowers... I do not know
whether to smile & thank you for them
or turn my face away, thinking,
what are flowers going to do?

petals shaped like little boats
but all they can do is drift.

out there, or perhaps in here,
the sun is setting. when its rays reach down
to pluck the last smiles from the last upturned faces,
you wonder why
I reach out my fingers to pluck the petals
from your flowers
& lay them on the sill.

you make as if to remove them, but I say,
leave them on the sill. I want to watch them
drift. while the wind shivers under the dark-spun cloak
of dusk, I hear you fidget beside me.
fidget because the shadows have silenced you
& silenced me, & there is nothing you can say.

finally, you get up & leave quietly, closing the door
behind you. I close my eyes
& it is almost as if
you were never here.
but when I look at the sill,
your flowers remain,
their petals drifting.
drifting. I smile at them & wonder
what can flowers ever do?

organism

it occurs to me again what a blind
   beast I am, we all are,
how life & its events flow over me with the ungraspable
   viscosity of
   water, & I'm this
     blind
       amorphous
    unseeing thing,
this floating skin on a tether,
   a dully throbbing
organ of nerves & blood vessels, & I'm not thinking about
      anything at all,
   just living, being carried forth
   like a
     speck
of foam on a wave. an inexorable wave
   beyond the edges of which
    I can't see,
blinded by water
     & I can't
  even see myself, or other people
    & I'm so very rarely awake.

but this I know:
   that I am not
    here
most of the time, & that there is no *I*
   (mirrors upon mirrors)
only a shifting sieve of sensations, of acquisitions, of defeats
   voicing meaningless words to the deaf air
    being deaf to the words
of others.

that we are all animals,
this I know—all so innocent & blind &
despicable, how we live continually in the state of the
new-born
our flesh a blood-filled
placenta pulsing
between ourselves
& the world. how helpless we are
& how oblivious.

this I know.

waiting (for dickinson)

time—that silent house of black leather—
where I stand—
by the empty cupboard of memory—
waiting to hear—
the midnight chimes.

coupling

supple couple all twined up,
silt-moist shine in white rope bound.
ropes of each other's arms & legs.
mouths open like pewter kegs.
pour me the wine, landlord, come over here,
survey your land: two people lost-found in each other,
drowning tomorrow, sifting sand.
measure the time of them: timeless,
hours of hours locked
unseemly in the dark;
open now to my wide eyes,
to the dwindling light,
to the shadow that lifts them
like a soft black kite.

four meditations (on silence & night)

i.

      you
like
      silence.
            you like
how it makes you
      feel. hollowed out like a
spoon, hungry.
      hungry but not
            wanting to
      eat.

ii.

silence (is) water.
it takes on the colour of whatever it is
      you
            feel—the shape
      of any container—the shape of your pain
or of your mouth
      or the inside of your head
even of your hands
& feet. it fills you until it is
      no longer itself, & you can
            hear all the voices
that whisper in kindness or in rage, but you
can't quite tell what they're saying, because they
      waver
            across
to you, heavy & almost colourless.

sound

                    in

water.

iii.

        you always think
the night must
        taste
                like glass—
        cold glass, clear
                & wet
                        with rain.
                (sweet on
        the tongue.)

        but suddenly
you realise
        it won't taste
                like that
        at all. because it's
blue—blue velvet—deep & swallowing &
        dark. (sometimes
                se-quin-ed
        with light.) & the night
won't taste like glass at all,
        if you were to
        run
                your
                        tongue
        along it.

it would taste of cloth.
        & that's what
the richest velvet tastes like,
          after all.
             rough
                   homespun.

iv.

night spills
        like black
             milk, cool &
        smooth
             to the taste.
        where you're waiting
             there I am.
bulb a harsh yellow moon
        you don't dare
to look at—marking this room with edges,
   a little white box you're
            trapped in.
                   (*patient.*)
        glint reflected off
             wooden desk. night outside,
        a foreign gentle ghost,
             eyeless.

        come here, caribou.
      don't be
             afraid.

Pooja Mittal was born in Lagos in 1983. Having lived in Nigeria, India and New Zealand, she has been widely published and anthologized in several countries. Her first book was published when she was 13, and at the age of 17, she was the youngest Featured Poet ever in the more than fifty-year history of *Poetry New Zealand*. She is the author of *Diaries of a Marked Man* and *Musings on Poetry*, both of which were published when she was 21 years old. In 2001, she was selected for UNESCO's international project, Babele Poetica, and in 2007, she was featured in both *The Best Australian Poetry 2007* and *The Best Australian Poems 2007*. Her poetry has been translated into Russian and performed at the Moscow International Poetry Festival. She lives in Melbourne, where she is completing her Ph.D at the Centre for Postcolonial Writing in Monash University.

www.ingramcontent.com/pod-product-compliance
Ingram Content Group Australia Pty Ltd
76 Discovery Rd, Dandenong South VIC 3175, AU
AUHW010631050325
407891AU00003B/20